Me and My Pet

RABBIT

Christine Morley and Carole Orbell

Illustrations by
Brita Granström

TWO CAN

In association with
FRANKLIN WATTS

Created by:
Two-Can Publishing Ltd
346 Old Street
London
EC1V 9NQ

Art Director: Carole Orbell
Senior Managing Editor: Christine Morley
Editor: Jennet Stott
Designer: Gareth Dobson
Research: Julia Hillyard
Consultant: Lisa Cobb, NCDL Animal Nurse of the Year 1995
Illustrator: Brita Granström
Photographer: John Englefield

'Two-Can' is a trademark of Two-Can Publishing Ltd.

This edition published in 1997 by Two-Can Publishing in association with:
Franklin Watts
96 Leonard Street
London
EC2A 4RH

Hardback ISBN: 1 85434 453 6

Dewey Decimal Classification 636.088

Hardback   2 4 6 8 10 9 7 5 3 1

A catalogue record for this book is available from the British Library.

Printed in Hong Kong by Wing King Tong

Contents

Furry friends

Everyone loves rabbits. They are cuddly, playful, and easy to take care of. But if you want to keep rabbits, you need to know how to care for these cute creatures properly.

Different rabbits

Rabbits have been around for thousands of years. Some live in the wild, while others live as pets in people's homes. Wild rabbits are small and brown, but pet rabbits can be many colours.

The first one to jump gets the lettuce.

Rabbits are lovable animals and they really enjoy being stroked.

Your own sweetheart

Many years ago, children called their pet rabbits "sweethearts" because they loved them so much. Show your rabbit you love her by stroking and talking to her.

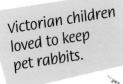

Victorian children loved to keep pet rabbits.

Country cousins

Wild rabbits live in the country in homes dug in the ground. These are called warrens and are made up of lots of rooms joined together by tunnels. Rabbits stay in the warren during the day and then come out to nibble on grass and plants in the early morning and evening, when it is quiet.

Girl rabbits burrow to make warrens.

Mmm, that grass looks very tasty.

Wild ways

Although pet rabbits are much friendlier than wild ones, they still do lots of things that wild rabbits do. They like to hop around nibbling grass, and they use their big ears and twitchy noses to sense what's around them.

All shapes and sizes

There are many beautiful types, or breeds, of rabbit around today. In fact, there are over 100. You can choose from cute little Dwarf rabbits to bunnies with thick, fluffy fur or large, floppy ears.

Some rabbits are too big for small hands to pick up.

Colourful coats

Pet rabbits come in a variety of gorgeous colours, from golden brown to black. Some are the same colour all over, while others have patches, spots and even stripes on their coats.

Little and large

Rabbits can be all sizes. The White Flemish Giant breed is bigger than some dogs, while Netherland Dwarf rabbits are tiny and weigh as little as a bag of sugar.

Dwarf rabbits like us are small and sweet!

Soft and smooth

All rabbits have soft fur to keep them warm. Some, such as Rex breeds, have short coats that feel like velvet. Angora rabbits have long, fluffy fur, often called wool. People use the wool to knit jumpers.

Show time

You can see different breeds of rabbits at a rabbit show. These are often run by rabbit clubs. To find a club near you, write to: British Rabbit Council, Purefoy House, 7 Kirkgate, Newark.

Big ears are best!

Most rabbits have long, upright ears. Some rabbits, called Lops, have floppy ears. Lops cannot hear as well as rabbits with upright ears.

Visit a rabbit show to see the bonniest bunnies.

The right rabbit

Before buying a rabbit, think about how much care, attention and space he will need. You will have to look after your rabbit all his life – which may be up to five years!

There's no way I'll fit in there.

Which breed?
It's important to think about what size of rabbit you want. Small- and medium-sized rabbits need less space than large rabbits, and they're easier to pick up too. If you want a young rabbit, make sure you know how big he will grow.

Long or short?
Long-haired rabbits look lovely, but they need more grooming than short-haired ones. Angora rabbits have coats that grow to a length of 12cm, so they need to be brushed every day to stop their fur getting tangled.

One or more?
Rabbits can get lonely, so keep more than one if you can. Girl rabbits get on well together, but boy rabbits will fight, unless they have grown up together and have plenty of space. Don't keep a boy and girl rabbit in the same cage, unless you want them to breed, or have babies.

Boy rabbits may fight if they live together.

Lonesome bunny

If you can't keep two rabbits, why not buy a guinea pig to keep your rabbit company? Guinea pigs and rabbits get along very well, but they need to be fed separately and put in their own hutches at night.

We may not be looking the same way...

...but we're best friends really!

Sisters will get along well with each other.

Are you ready?

Before you bring your bunny home, make sure you have a comfortable home for her. She will need a roomy hutch, tasty food, plenty of water and lots of hugs!

No place like home

Rabbits are usually kept outside in a house called a hutch. You can buy one from a pet shop, or ask an adult to make one. It must be big enough for your rabbit to move about in and to stand up in. It should be raised off the floor and divided into two rooms: one to use in the day, the other to sleep in.

This is the best-kept hutch in town.

Make sure your rabbit has lots of clean straw and fresh food.

1 water bottle
2 newspapers
3 straw
4 hay rack

A happy hutch

Rabbits don't like very hot or very cold weather, so put the hutch somewhere that's sheltered from the wind, the rain and the hot sun.

I'm as snug as a bug in a rug.

Food and water

Inside the hutch, you will need a hay rack and a water bottle to keep your rabbit's food and water clean. The bottom of the hutch should be lined with newspaper and covered by wood chippings or cat litter. Finally, add plenty of fresh straw to keep your bunny snug.

Blankets will keep a bunny cosy in winter.

Rabbits like to hear friendly chatter, so keep the hutch very close to your home.

The great indoors

You can also keep your rabbit inside your house. You will need a special cage for her to sleep in and you will have to make sure she has a safe area to run around in. Turn to page 20 to find out more.

Choosing your chum

Most rabbits are cuddly and cute, and you'll probably want every one you see. But before you buy, here are a few tips on how to find and choose a healthy rabbit.

The best bunny

A healthy rabbit should have a clean, shiny coat and bright eyes. Look under his tail and in his ears to see if they're clean, and check that his claws are not too long.

When you buy a rabbit

When you have found a rabbit you like, find out if it's a boy or girl. If you want more than one rabbit, ask if there are any from the same family for sale.

Home and dry

Take your rabbit home in a strong carrying box with air holes in it, so that your rabbit can breathe. Try not to jiggle him about, and keep your journey as short as possible.

Settling in

When you bring your rabbit home, he may feel scared. Make sure his hutch is comfortable and give him fresh food and water. Leave him to explore his new home, but come back often to check he's happy.

Take your time choosing your rabbit from a good pet shop.

Hop to the shop

A pet shop is the usual place to buy a rabbit. However, if you want a special breed, such as an Angora, you may need to go to a breeder. You can find one through a rabbit club or rabbit magazine.

Let your new rabbit settle in before your friends crowd around.

Feeling hungry

Pet rabbits spend most of their days nibbling, just like wild ones! Give your bunny plenty of fresh food and clean water every day to keep her happy and full of energy.

Never feed a rabbit plants with pesticides on them.

1 pear
2 turnip
3 celery
4 cucumber
5 mushrooms
6 peas
7 tomato

Food for free

Dandelions, chickweed and clover can be found in the garden and are good for rabbits. But always ask an adult if you have pulled up the right plants, because some, such as bindweed, are poisonous.

Magic mix

Every morning, give your rabbit fresh fruit and vegetables with about half a cup of pellets or cereals. This mix of food should give your rabbit all the goodness she needs. Some hay at night helps your rabbit's digestion.

Crisp and crunchy

Lettuce, broccoli and other types of greens make a good evening snack for your rabbit. But don't give her too much lettuce, as it can cause diarrhoea.

More or less?

If your bunny gobbles up everything quickly, you could give her a little more. If your pet always leaves food uneaten, cut down on how much you give her. Always take away food that is left, or it will rot.

Keep bunnies away from vegetable patches!

What a feast! Is it my birthday?

Neat and tidy

Rabbits keep their coats clean and shiny all by themselves. But if you give them a gentle brush regularly, it will get them used to being handled. They really enjoy it too!

Keeping clean

Watch your rabbit to see how he cleans himself. He uses his front teeth to pick out bits of dirt and then licks his coat with his tongue. This covers his fur with oil, which protects it. To clean his face, first he licks his paws, then he wipes them over his ears.

Rabbits like to wash themselves several times a day.

Now where did I put that mirror?

Hair care

Short-haired rabbits can be brushed once a week. Gently brush the fur towards the tail – don't forget the tummy. Long-haired rabbits need to be brushed every day to stop their fur getting tangled.

Your hair could do with a brush too!

Up and away

To groom your rabbit properly, you need to know how to pick him up safely. Put one hand in front of him, then slide the other hand under his back legs. Hold him close along your arm or with his head over your shoulder. Never lift your rabbit up by his ears or legs.

Is this what's called a bunny hug?

Winter coat

In the winter, your rabbit grows a thick coat to keep him warm. As the weather turns warmer, he loses this coat. This is called moulting. Regular brushing helps to remove loose hairs when your rabbit is moulting.

Never bath your bunny as this will wash out the special oil in his coat.

Going down

To put your rabbit down, turn him around so he faces away from you and put down his back feet first. This way, your bunny cannot kick out and scratch you if he gets frightened.

Keeping fit

Playing with your rabbit is great fun and helps keep her fit, too. Let your bunny play outside as much as possible, but keep her in a run, so that you can catch her again!

Run rabbit run!
If you build a run next to your rabbit's hutch, she can hop around whenever she feels like it. Make sure the fence goes into the ground, or that the bottom of the run is covered with wire mesh, so your rabbit can't dig under it.

Garden games
You can let your rabbit play in a garden, as long as there is a strong fence around it. Watch out for cats or dogs that might scare your rabbit.

A good game to play is to bury food for your bunny to sniff out and dig up.

So this is what it's like in a submarine.

A long piece of pipe is safe and fun for rabbits to explore.

I don't need ice-cream to stay cool.

Moving around

Ask an adult to make a triangular-shaped run that can be moved around the garden. This way your rabbit can nibble fresh grass every day. Remember to leave a bowl of water in the run and keep it shaded from the sun.

A colourful painted plant pot makes a great toy for a rabbit.

Hard to catch

Your rabbit will enjoy being outdoors in a run and sometimes won't want to go back into her hutch! You will have to be very patient and shoo her into a corner. Never run after her or grab her – she'll only get more scared and difficult to catch.

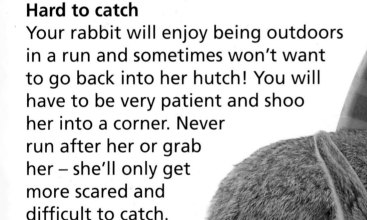

Indoor bunny

If you don't have a garden, your rabbit will be quite happy living indoors. Just make sure he spends most of the day out of his cage, hopping around the house.

Always watch your bunny – he could get into dangerous spots!

Hutch-free zone

You won't need a hutch for your indoor bunny. Instead, a large wire cage will do as his bedroom at night. During the day, your rabbit should run free or have a large play-pen to explore.

Playing safe

To make your home safe, hide sharp objects, such as scissors, and move electrical wires which your rabbit might chew. Close all doors so he can't wander into unsafe places.

Rabbits love company and like to feel part of the family.

Keep dogs on leads or they might frighten your rabbit.

Bad bunny

Sometimes your rabbit will do naughty things, such as chewing your favourite toy, or going to the toilet on the carpet. If you catch him misbehaving, say "No" firmly and squirt him with water from a spray bottle. Never smack your rabbit or shout at him.

Toilet training

A rabbit can be trained to use a litter tray as a toilet. Line the tray with newspaper and cover it with wood shavings or cat litter. If you put your rabbit in the tray after he's eaten, he'll soon learn to use it himself.

Ooops! I'm not supposed to kick the sawdust.

With a little training, your bunny can use a litter tray.

Routine care

Your rabbit likes her home to be cleaned every day. Keep her hutch nice and fresh by taking away uneaten food and dirty bedding.

1 bottle brushes
2 dustpan and brush
3 scrubbing brush
4 rubber gloves
5 bucket
6 soap
7 scraper

Cleaning kit

You will need all the items shown here when cleaning out the hutch. Remember to wear rubber gloves when picking up dirty bedding. And only use disinfectant that's made for animals – you can buy this from pet shops.

Now that's clean.

Dirt busters!

Replace dirty or wet bedding daily with clean, dry wood chippings and straw. Once a week, sweep the hutch then rinse it with hot, soapy water and spray it with animal disinfectant. Always make sure the hutch is completely dry before putting your rabbit back in.

Rabbit droppings and dirty straw can be put on a compost heap.

Bottles and bowls

Every day, empty and wash the food bowl and water bottle. Once a week, you should give the bottle, lid and tube a good scrub. You can buy special long brushes for this job.

When you go on holiday, leave your rabbit in safe hands.

Bon voyage!

When you go on holiday, find a friend or neighbour to care for your bunny. Before you go, clean out the hutch and make sure there is plenty of food and bedding. Write down a list of things that your carer must do, as well as what food your bunny likes and dislikes. Remember to leave your vet's telephone number and address.

Bunny talk

The noises and movements your rabbit makes are his way of talking to you. As you get to know your rabbit, you'll be able to tell when he's hungry, when he wants to play, and when he's feeling tired.

When your bunny licks your finger it means he really likes you.

All sorts of smells
Your rabbit's nose will twitch madly when other rabbits are around. This is because he recognises them by their smell. Sometimes he will rub his scent on other rabbits. This way, he knows that they're his friends.

On the scent
To be friendly your rabbit will rub his head against you, or he'll lick your hands and fingers with his tongue. This leaves a special scent on you that only rabbits and other animals can smell.

You smell just like me!

Danger signals

Wild rabbits have to keep watch for dangerous animals. Pet rabbits do this, too. If they see or hear something strange, they rise up on their back legs to get a better view. If they sense danger, they thump their back legs. This is a signal for other rabbits to run to safety.

Rabbits are shy and sometimes they will hide from people.

Wild rabbits wag their tails as a warning.

Cross bunnies

When rabbits are cross they will stare straight at each other and scratch the ground with their front paws. They will also stamp their back feet and may even try to bite each other!

Watch the TV, not me!

Check-up

Pet rabbits usually stay in good condition, as long as they are properly cared for. Help to keep your rabbit healthy by carrying out the checks on this page.

Use an old pair of kitchen scales to weigh your rabbit.

I must cut down on those carrots!

Weekly weigh-in
It's a good idea to weigh your rabbit every week and write down her weight. If she's become much heavier or lighter, she may be ill. If she puts on weight every week, she might not be getting enough exercise.

Visiting the vet

When you first buy your bunny, take her to the vet for a check-up. The vet will give your rabbit injections to stop her catching nasty illnesses, such as myxomatosis. The vet can also perform an operation on your rabbit to stop her (or him) breeding. This is called neutering.

Check your rabbit's claws every month in case they're overgrown.

I wonder if that tickles?

Clipping claws

If your rabbit's claws grow too long, your vet will trim them. She may even trim your rabbit's teeth, too!

Your vet will look at your bunny's teeth to see if they are too long.

Droppings for dinner!

Don't worry if you see your rabbit eating her own droppings. It may sound very strange to us, but it is quite normal for rabbits! They do it because these droppings still have lots of nutrients left in them.

Feeling poorly

Just like people, rabbits get sick from time to time. Unlike people, they can't tell you when they're feeling bad. So here are a few warning signs to watch out for.

Sick or not?

When your rabbit is sick, he will probably stop eating and running around, although he may drink a lot. You should telephone the vet and she will tell you whether your rabbit needs to go to the surgery.

Aaaitchoo!

Rabbits can catch a disease that is similar to a cold. It is called snuffles. A rabbit with snuffles has a runny nose and sometimes runny eyes. If your rabbit has these symptoms, call the vet quickly.

These fleas are making me hopping mad.

Hop off!

If your bunny starts scratching a lot, look closely in his fur and see if you can spot any tiny, dark specks. These are fleas. Ask an adult to puff flea powder on your rabbit, and spray the hutch with flea spray too.

Making a note

When you visit your vet, she'll want to know some things about your rabbit's health, such as his age and weight, and what illnesses or injections he has had. Keep this information in a notebook, so that you won't forget anything.

Take a photo of your bunny to put in your notebook.

Bunnies galore

Everyone loves baby rabbits, but if you decide to breed from your rabbit, make sure that you can find good homes for all of the babies.

Making a nest
It will be about one month before the doe gives birth. At this time, make her hutch warm and comfortable with soft straw. She will pull out some of her own fur to make her nest extra snug.

Does and bucks
To breed rabbits put a doe (girl rabbit) and a buck (boy rabbit) into a hutch for five or six days. After this time, put the doe back in her own cage as she might fight with the buck.

Babies drink their mother's milk for the first six weeks.

A mother rabbit will need extra food.

Kitten care

After two days, take a peek at the kittens to see if they're moving – that means they are healthy. But don't pick them up until they're three weeks old, as you may upset the mother.

A new family

Your rabbit will probably have her babies at night or early in the morning when it is quiet. You will be excited to see the babies, which are called kittens, but you must not touch the nest for a few days. If you do, the doe may become frightened and attack her kittens.

Even babies like me know how to keep clean.

Friendly owners

The kittens will be ready to leave their mum when they are about seven weeks old. By this time, they will be eating the same food as a grown-up rabbit. You must try to find good homes for all of them. Why not ask your friends if they would like a baby rabbit to keep?

Useful words

agouti A type of wild rabbit with brown, speckled fur. Other rabbits with the same type of speckled fur are said to have agouti fur.

booster These are injections that your rabbit needs to have every year to protect him against diseases.

breed A special type of rabbit, such as a Dutch or an Angora.

breeding When a boy and girl rabbit mate, so they can have baby rabbits.

buck A boy, or male, rabbit.

crossbreed A rabbit whose parents or grandparents are different breeds, or a mixture of breeds.

doe A girl, or female, rabbit.

kitten A baby or young rabbit.

litter A group of baby rabbits from the same family.

neutering An operation for male and female rabbits to keep them from breeding, or having babies.

pedigree or purebreed Rabbits whose parents, grandparents, and great-grandparents are all the same breed. They will have a special certificate to prove this.

pregnancy The time when the mother carries her babies inside her. This is usually between 28 and 31 days for a rabbit.

vaccinations These are injections that rabbits have to keep them from catching diseases from other animals.

warren The underground tunnels and burrows where wild rabbits live.